the art of group talk

HOW TO LEAD
BETTER CONVERSATIONS
WITH TEENAGE GIRLS

"Why are my parents trying to
make my life so miserable?"
AMBER, 8TH GRADE

———

"I have a prayer request.
I killed my hamster."
JESSICA, 11TH GRADE

———

"I think you may have just
shared a little too much."
SASHA, 7TH GRADE

———

"Do we have to be vegans in heaven?
That's what I heard."

EMILY, 6TH GRADE

———

"I'm not sure what I think about God,
but I feel like it's okay for me to say
that out loud here."

CAROLINE, 12TH GRADE

———

The Art of Group Talk: Teen Girls
Published by Orange, a division of The reThink Group, Inc.
5870 Charlotte Lane, Suite 300
Cumming, GA 30040 U.S.A.

The Orange logo is a registered trademark of The reThink Group, Inc.

All Scripture quotations, unless otherwise noted, are taken from the Holy Bible, New International Version®. NIV®. Copyright © 1973, 1978, 1984 by International Bible Society. Used by permission of Zondervan.

Other Orange products are available online and direct from the publisher. Visit our website at www.ThinkOrange.com for more resources like these.

ISBN: 978-1-63570-079-4

©2018 The reThink Group, Inc.

Authors: Ashley Bohinc, Crystal Chiang
Lead Editor: Afton Phillips
Contributing Writers: Steph Whitacre
Lead Small Editing Team: Mike Jeffries,
Sara Shelton, Adriana Howard, Steph Whitacre
Art Direction: Ryan Boon
Project Manager: Nate Brandt
Design: FiveStone

Printed in the United States of America
Third Edition 2018

3 4 5 6 7 8 9 10 11 12

10/08/18

Table of Contents

Foreword

This is a book about how to have better conversations with teenage girls.

Because, as a small group leader, you lead a conversation with teenage girls every single week. Conversations about . . .
their lives.
their dreams.
their friends.
their more-than-friends.
and their definitely-not friends.

And sometimes, you even manage to lead conversations about faith.

This is a book to remind you that your small group conversations—even the ones that don't go exactly as planned—**really matter.**

But there are a few ways to make your conversations **matter even more.**

create a safe place

clarify their faith as they grow

Introduction

You probably signed up to be a small group leader
(or SGL for short) because you wanted . . .
to make a big difference.
to change the world.
to invest in a few teenage girls so you could help them
develop a lifelong, authentic kind of faith.

We call that **leading small**.

Maybe you didn't know exactly what you were getting into
when you signed up to be an SGL, but you probably at
least knew this:

**Leading a small group means leading a weekly small
group conversation.**

Kind of obvious, right?

But the truth is that figuring out how to lead a conversation
with a group of teenage girls isn't always obvious. It's
definitely not like leading a conversation with a group
of adults.

I (Crystal) learned this the hard way. When I signed up to
be an SGL, I had some pretty big expectations for how
those weekly small group conversations should look. At
the time, I thought leading a small group of teenage girls
would be pretty much like leading a conversation with a
bunch of me's—but shorter, louder, and better dressed.

Before I became an SGL, I expected to lead small group conversations where every girl . . .
paid attention.
participated.
cried.
asked deep theological questions.
decided to devote themselves to full-time ministry.
read the Bible every day just because they wanted to.

^ attempted to lead
But then I ~~led~~ my first small group of ninth grade girls and, well, you can guess how that went. I remember feeling like I was at a zoo where someone had left all the cages open. Most days getting them to sit in an actual circle without shrieking like hyenas was a win.

If you've been an SGL for more than five minutes, then you already know what I've learned—that leading a conversation with a group of teenage girls doesn't always live up to your expectations. (Especially if your expectations looked anything like mine.)

If you have any SGL experience whatsoever, it's probably safe to say **you know what it's like to have a small group conversation totally bomb.**

Maybe you led a small group where your girls weren't exactly talkative.
You tried to get the conversation moving, but you were met with . . .
the sound of crickets.
blank stares.
the backs of their phones as they tried a new Instagram filter.

Or maybe they were a little *too* talkative.
Maybe you had to scream the discussion questions at the
top of your lungs while they . . .
made plans for the following weekend.
watched a viral YouTube video.
asked you to judge their impromptu talent show.

Or maybe they were just the right amount of talkative, but
you're convinced volunteer training didn't prepare you for
the kinds of topics they wanted to talk about.

When leading a small group of teenage girls, sometimes
you have to beg them to say something—anything.

Other times, you wish they would all instantly get laryngitis
at the same time.

And more often than you'd like, you probably head home
after a particularly challenging small group and wonder,
"Did I say the right thing?
Were they even listening?
Do these conversations matter at all?"

If you've ever been there, you're not alone. Everyone who
has ever led a small group of teenage girls has, at some
point, wondered if they were completely wasting their
time. (We don't exactly have the statistical data to support
this claim, but we're pretty sure it's true.)

Especially on days when your group spends more time
taking selfies and looking out the window for boys than
engaging in a conversation about faith—those questions
are understandable.

But the next time a conversation goes completely off the
rails and you wonder if you're a terrible small group leader
(or if leading a small group of teenage girls should be
classified as a new form of torture), there are two things we
hope you'll remember.

Here's the first:
Your small group conversations matter.

And we don't just mean those once-in-a-lifetime conversations where everyone cries and hugs and gets saved (again). We mean every small group conversation.

The one with way too many awkward silences? It mattered.
The one where you didn't get through a single discussion question? It mattered.
The one where your group wanted to know if God could make a mozzarella stick so hot that even He couldn't eat it? It mattered.
And the conversation you're about to lead this week? Yep. It's going to matter too.

The good news for SGLs like you and me is that the quality and effectiveness of the conversation you'll lead this week won't determine your ultimate success or failure as a small group leader. Sometimes a conversation will bomb, and that's okay, because that one conversation isn't the only conversation you'll ever have with your few.

In the book *Lead Small*, we talked about the importance of showing up predictably—weekly, in fact—for your few. Actually, it's the very first thing we talked about. That's because showing up predictably, consistently, and regularly in the lives of the teenage girls you lead is the foundation of leading your small group (and of leading a small group conversation).

I (Crystal) lead a group of sophomore girls, and I have to admit that last year, when they were freshmen, I had more of those "Does this even matter?" moments than I could count. As someone who creates small group resources for a living, I thought, "I should be better at this! Our conversations should be *better* than this!" It really wasn't until summer camp—a whole year after our group started—that I began to see a turn in our conversations.

They became more honest and less awkward. Part of it was my girls were growing up and less interested in cartwheel contests during small group, but another part was that it took an entire year of not-so-awesome group talks for the girls to learn to trust me and trust each other enough to have real conversations.

When you show up predictably, you begin to understand that one conversation doesn't determine your success as a small group leader. Your success is actually determined by every small group conversation you've ever had, added up and then multiplied by factors we haven't yet identified. When you combine the dozens, or hundreds, or thousands of conversations you've had with your small group, they equal something pretty significant. They equal . . .
Relationships.
Trust.
Influence.

I (Ashley) am still in contact with girls who were in my middle school small group nine years ago. Many times we laugh uncontrollably at the things they remember. I am reminded often that even though we talked about many important topics like friendships, boys, decision-making, forgiveness, and, most importantly, Jesus, they also remember me talking about how much I love butterflies and putting on new socks. There are days I wonder if I was a good SGL. But then I remember how each of those girls came to me a few years down the road when they were in high school because they were going through difficult situations. They trusted me and leaned on me because they believed I was a safe place, and that I was for them. And maybe even better, they trusted and leaned on each other. The sum of the small, relational deposits made over their three years in middle school— even the non-spiritual ones—added up to something more significant than I could have ever imagined.

So you see, your small group conversations matter— even the ones that are difficult, or frustrating, or don't exactly go according to plan. They matter because each of those weekly small group conversations is part of something bigger.

Ten years from now, the girls in your small group will probably not remember much of what was said during your small group conversations, but they will remember how those consistent, weekly conversations resulted in relationships that made an impact on their lives. It may even cue them to go looking for those kinds of meaningful relationships again. That's the power of showing up consistently.

So next time a small group conversation doesn't quite meet your expectations, remember: **your small group conversations matter—maybe more than you think.**

But here's the second thing we hope you remember:

Your small group conversations can matter more.

In fact, that's what this book is all about—practical ideas and strategies to help you make the most of your conversations with your small group.

While the one conversation you lead this week will not determine your success as a small group leader, it will affect it. The influence you're building through your weekly conversations is important, but if you never actually use that influence to help your few build a more authentic faith, then you'll have missed it.

But you're not going to miss it. We know that because you're reading a book about how to make your small group conversations matter more, and that's a pretty good sign. You're already on your way to leading better conversations—ones in which the girls in your group will not only be able to engage, but will be able to . . .
be themselves.
share their doubts.

ask tough questions.
share their struggles.

It isn't always easy to lead those kinds of conversations, though. So if you've ever looked at your small group of teenage girls and wished you knew . . .
what to say
what not to say
what to ask
how to ask it
when to speak
when to listen
how to make them talk
how to make them stop talking
. . . then keep reading.

We don't know everything about leading conversations for teenage girls, but we've spent a lot of time leading small groups, talking to other small group leaders, and learning the art of group talk. And now we want to take the things we've learned and share them with you. Things that we hope will help you make the most of your limited opportunities to lead a conversation with your small group.

So remember.

Your small group conversations matter. They matter because with every conversation you lead, you're building influence, trust, and relationships with your few that have the potential to influence them for a lifetime.

But your small group conversations can matter more.
And here's how . . .

1

chapter
one
prepare

Prepare

Picture this.

You just got out of work. It's been a long day. Nobody told you that you were going to have your picture taken. Your hair was out of control. Plus, your lunch meeting required you to talk so much you couldn't eat your food, so now you're starving.

But the day is finally over!

You head to your car. Beyoncé is on the radio (win!). As you pull out of the parking lot, all you can think about is getting home, putting on sweats, and relaxing. Then you remember that tonight's small group. So, instead of heading home, you . . .
race to a drive thru,
scarf down a taco,
drop by the house to let your dog out,
swing by a coffee shop and *pray* the caffeine kicks in,
screech into the parking lot right on time,
greet Jana, Jenna, and Jayna as they walk in (and try to remember which is which),
and begin to catch up with your few.

Finally, when the music starts to cue the beginning of worship, you realize that *you have no idea what you're supposed to be talking about tonight.*

Ever been there? We sure have. Don't get us wrong. We love our small groups. We care about them. We're committed to them. We want to have great conversations together. But . . . well, we're not always as prepared for our conversations as we should be.

Maybe you can relate. Maybe you know what it's like to fly through the church doors, desperately searching your phone for the email from your student pastor about what in the world you were supposed to talk about in small group. During the message, you tried to skim through the discussion questions, but you found it hard to concentrate with your student pastor talking so much. Then when you got to small group, you realized you didn't really hear much of the message and you couldn't *exactly* remember all the small group questions, so you read them from your phone until one of your girls reminded you, "Um, those are the questions we answered *last* week."

If we're honest, we've all had weeks like that. It happens. If you've been with your group for some time, they might not have even noticed how much you were winging it. But on your way home, you might have wondered, *What kind of conversation could we have had if I'd been just a little more prepared?*

If you want to get serious about making your conversations with your few matter more (and we know that you do), then we've got to talk about **preparation**. That's why the first step in leading a better small group conversation is to . . .

PREPARE

We know.

You're a volunteer. You don't get paid to lead a small group. You've inserted yourself into the tumultuous lives of a few teenage girls, and you're going to get absolutely nothing in return, except maybe a free T-shirt and some sub-standard pizza. You're already giving a *ton* of your time by showing up and leading these conversations, and now we're suggesting you spend <u>more</u> time preparing for those conversations?

Well, yes. But it's simple. We promise!

There are four things you can do to prepare for your small group conversations each week. And you can do them all from your couch.

If you want to prepare for your small group conversation, READ your email.

We know that email is outdated. (That's why we created the Lead Small app.*) That's what our small groups tell us anyway. But we're not teenage girls. We're grown-ups. And grown-ups check their email.

We don't mean those emails about buy-one-get-one jeans or free shipping this weekend. Those emails probably won't help you prepare for your small group (although you should probably bookmark them just in case).

We're talking about the weekly communication your student pastor sends you through email, the Lead Small app, a Facebook group, or by carrier pigeon.

We may not know your student pastor, but we're going to assume a few things about what they do every week. We're guessing your student pastor, youth director, or coach . . .
cares about your small group conversation.
thinks about your small group conversation.
has a plan for your small group conversation.
sends you the plan for your small group conversation.

Hopefully, that communication from your student pastor tells you important information like **what *they'll* be**

---

* Find out more at LeadSmall.org.

teaching and **what *you'll* be asking** in small group each week.

Ring any bells?
No?

Then you probably need to update your contact information in the church database or check your Recently Deleted folder.

But if you've checked, and double checked and are absolutely positive your student pastor doesn't communicate with you weekly, try not to be too hard on them. We're sure they really want you to succeed as a small group leader!

So don't get mad. If your student pastor doesn't send you a weekly email, try this . . .

1. Open your email app.
2. Write a new message to your student pastor.
3. Say something like this:

> Hey _____! I've been thinking about how to continually improve group time with my girls. I was thinking it would be awesome to get an email every week—maybe a few days in advance—that helps me get ready for my small group. My girls are crazy, and I think my small group conversations could be a lot better if I had a little time to think about what we're teaching and read my small group questions beforehand. Is that something that would be possible? Thanks for everything you do. You're awesome!

Pretty simple, right?

And if your student pastor already sends you a weekly update, then your job is even easier:

1. Open your email, app, or window (for the carrier pigeon).
2. Read it.

If you already do this, way to go! You are a very prepared SGL. And hey, here's a thought: If you love getting those emails in advance, take a second to hit "Reply" to your student pastor's weekly email and say, "Thanks for sending this!" They'll love to hear their weekly emails aren't disappearing into inbox oblivion.

If you want this week's small group conversation to matter more, then you need to know what the small group conversation will be about—you know, *before* you walk in the door.

Prepare for your small group conversation.
READ YOUR EMAIL.

If you want to prepare for your small group conversation, REHEARSE what you'll say.

Have you ever had an **imaginary conversation?**

Sure you have. Maybe it was when you were . . .
getting ready for a first date.
preparing for a tough conversation with your boss.
thinking of some killer comebacks for that troll on Facebook.

Having imaginary conversations simply means mentally rehearsing what you're going to say before you say it. Imaginary conversations are helpful when you're preparing for a date, and they're also helpful when you're preparing for your not-so-imaginary small group conversations, too.

We're not saying you should memorize lines or write a monologue for your small group conversation. In fact, please don't. That's weird. We're just saying that **what you say can probably be said better if you rehearse what you're going to say (or not say) before you say it.**

Just like . . .
a teacher practices before taking on a classroom
of students
a hair stylist practices before actually cutting a human's hair
a professional musician practices before the big show
. . . you should practice for your small group conversation.

As an SGL, having an imaginary conversation means trying to anticipate how your small group conversation will go *before* small group so you'll be less likely to be caught off-guard *during* small group.

So how do you do that? Well, once you've read your email from your student pastor, ask yourself a few questions about **what they'll be teaching** like . . .
- What do my girls know, think, or feel about this topic?
- How does this topic relate to specific situations in their lives right now?
- How will _____ respond or feel when we talk about this?

Next, take a look at your small group questions for the week, and ask yourself a few questions about **what you'll be discussing** like . . .
- Will these small group questions make sense to them?
- How are my girls going to answer these questions?
- Will they feel comfortable answering them honestly?
- Do I need to rephrase any of these questions for my group?
- Is there anyone in my group I need to connect with beforehand?

See? It's simple, but it's so important!

When you have a weekly imaginary conversation with yourself, you'll be able to better . . .
clarify your thoughts.
refine your words.
anticipate their responses.
lead the conversation.

Maybe this week you'll be talking about going through difficult times, and you know one of your girl's grandma just passed away, and she is a mess about it. Connecting with her prior to group will help her prepare her emotions so she has a better chance of engaging with the group in a way that's beneficial and includes the group in what she's experiencing.

Or maybe you will be talking about sexual integrity, and you know one of the girls in your group was sexually abused in her past. Because this is such a sensitive topic, you want to make sure she has a heads up on what the questions will be, and confirm that she feels comfortable.

Remember, if you want this week's small group conversation to matter more, you want to think about how the conversation will go *before* the conversation begins.

Prepare for your small group conversation.
REHEARSE WHAT YOU'LL SAY.

If you want to prepare for your small group conversation, PACK a survival kit.

No, we don't mean bandages and disinfectant (although, with teenagers, that's actually not a bad idea).

We mean the kind of supplies that will help you rescue your small group conversation in the event of emergencies like . . .
out-of-control talkers.
awkward silences.
irrelevant rabbit trails.
general chaos.

 We'll talk about how to use these supplies later in this book. **Just look for this symbol.** For now, just trust us. You'll need:

- A confetti popper
- A stack of icebreaker questions
- A noisemaker
- A stress ball
- A deck of cards
- A zipper lock bag
- Pens
- Paper
- Tissues (*Note:* You're leading teenage girls, so maybe pack twice the amount you think is necessary.)

Remember, if you want this week's small group conversation to matter more, you want to be ready for anything.

**Prepare for your small group conversation.
PACK A SURVIVAL KIT.**

If you want to prepare for your small group conversation, PRAY for your few.

If you're anything like us, praying for your small group is, unfortunately, sometimes more of an afterthought than a vital part of your weekly preparation. Some weeks, you may only manage a hurried, well-intentioned plea to God on the way to small group. Other weeks, the only time you pray for your few is *during* your small group.

But no matter how many times you've prayed for your few in the last week, month, or year, we've discovered there are at least two reasons why praying for your small group should be an every week kind of thing.

Pray for your few because *they* need it. Being a teenage girl is hard. Like, really hard. Besides school, sports, drama, breakups, gossip, parents, siblings, and everything else your small group is dealing with, every teenage girl is also wrestling with big questions about who they are, why they matter, what they believe, and who they'll become. That's a lot for any teenager to manage. So as you prepare for your small group each week, don't forget to pray for your few. They need it.

(And when you pray for your few, don't hesitate to send them a text to let them know you were thinking about them. No matter how old you are, it's always nice to hear somebody's praying for you.)

But there's another reason you should pray for your few.

Pray for your few because *you* need it. When you pray for someone else, it's usually because you want God to do something for *them*. But what if, when God told us to pray for each other (which He did quite often), He had a second purpose in mind? What if He designed prayer in such a way that praying for the other person didn't just result in change for *them*? What if it changes *us*, too?

When we pray for someone else, we learn to . . .
consider their needs.
imagine their world.
feel their emotions.
understand their perspective.

One of the most helpful things you can do is pray for a kid (or parent or co-leader) you *don't* like that much, because you need God to change your heart toward them. In other words, **when you pray for the teenagers you lead, you develop more compassion for them.** And as an SGL, you'll need that compassion when . . .
the conversation gets awkward.
someone rolls their eyes.
they ask a tough question.
confidentiality gets broken.

As you prepare for your small group this week, don't let prayer be an afterthought. Be intentional about it. Maybe that means you . . .
pray for a few girls each day.
write their names on your calendar.
set reminders in your phone.

However you decide to remind yourself, make praying for your few a habit. Remember, if you want this week's small group conversation to matter more, you want to have a conversation with God *before* you have a conversation with your few.

Prepare for your small group conversation.
PRAY FOR YOUR FEW.

So there you have it. Four ways to **prepare** for your small group conversation every week. We said it would be simple, right?
Read your email.
Rehearse what you'll say.
Pack a survival kit.
Pray for your few.

And now that you're (mostly) prepared for your small group conversation, let's talk about how to lead that conversation.

QUIZ:

HOW WELL DO YOU PREPARE FOR YOUR SMALL GROUP?

Throughout this book, you'll find a few quizzes we've created as self-evaluation tools. Circle your answers (or just think them), and at the end of this book, you'll be able to see which areas of group conversation you're stellar at, as well as the areas where you might have a little room to grow.

Answer honestly, and have fun!

Did you get an email from your student pastor this week? Did you read it?

Yes   No   Um, I don't know.

Do you pray for your few regularly? You know, other than the times they're crying in front of you about their latest break-up?

Yes   No   Define *regularly*.

QUIZ

Do you have a system for reminding yourself to pray for your few?

Yes   No   I don't need reminders.
                               I'm amazing.

Do you usually know what your conversation is going to be about before you arrive?

Yes   No   Why ruin the surprise?

Do you know the topic so well that you could lead your small group conversation with your eyes closed? Well, we're not saying you should, because that would be weird. But could you navigate most of the conversation without looking at your small group questions?

Yes   No   Sometimes

NEXT STEP

We know the art of group talk looks a little different for everyone. Below, write one or two specific and practical things you can do to better PREPARE to lead your few this week.

_____

_____

_____

_____

_____

_____

_____

_____

_____

_____

_____

NEXT STEP

2

chapter
two
connect

Connect

(Talk about something FUN)

Now that you've . . .
read your email
rehearsed what you'll say
packed your survival kit
prayed for your few
. . . you're ready! It's time to finally lead a
small group conversation.

But wait.

What about the girls in your group?
Are *they* ready for your conversation?

Right now, the teenage girls you lead are probably *not*
thinking about your next small group conversation.
More than likely, they're thinking about . . .
their big science test tomorrow,
how they're going to get ungrounded,
who's going to be at practice tonight,
how many people commented on their last post,
or, if they're in high school, how many hours they have to
work to pay for gas money and concert tickets.

We don't mean to discourage you. It's not that your few
don't care about you, your small group, or their faith. It's
just that they have a lot of other things on their minds.

And that's okay! You don't need your few to come to small
group ready to talk *only* about forgiveness, prayer, or the

book of Ephesians. You need them to come to small group ready to talk about *anything*—especially the stuff that matters to them . . . even if that thing is how many likes their latest selfie is getting.

In the first few minutes of your small group conversation, your few don't need to immediately dive into that week's discussion questions. **They just need to connect.**

Don't forget that leading a small group is about something much bigger than discussion questions. It's about the relationships you're building over time. But you'll never build a great small group relationship—or have a great small group conversation—if you can't connect first.

How you connect with your small group is simple. For an SGL like you, it may even be obvious. But just so we're all on the same page, let's put it this way:

Before you talk about faith with your small group, you should spend a little time talking about their week.

Before you ask them to be vulnerable, you should probably ask what they're doing this weekend.

And before you tell them to participate, you should make sure they know you're happy to see them.

Here's the point:
Before a teenage girl can ENGAGE in a conversation about a *God* who cares about her, she may need to CONNECT with *people* who care about her.

2.1

If you want your small group conversations to matter more,

connect with them

Connect with them

If you're leading a small group of teenage girls, you're probably not a teenager or you won't be one for much longer. You may have been one at some point, but I'm guessing you're not anymore. And since you're not a teenage girl, it's probably not always going to be easy to connect with the students in your group.

That's because they're not like you. Chances are, at no point today did you have to ask someone if you could go to the bathroom. You probably didn't have to "try out" for anything. And more than likely attending a dance in your school cafeteria-turned-ballroom didn't even cross your mind. Whether it's the music you listen to, the things you worry about, or the number of emojis you text each day, you and your few are very different people. At least, I hope so, because they're teenage girls, and you're not.

And they're not like you used to be. You may remember what it was like to be a teenage girl, but things aren't like they were when you were their age. Whether you're in your eighties or your twenties, the world has changed quite a bit since you were a teenager. Sure, you had your share of awkward moments as a teenager, but can you imagine having lived with the possibility those moments would be recorded, distributed, or even live-streamed? Maybe you were bullied or teased, but can you imagine never being able to escape it because, thanks to social media, the conversation never ends? Maybe you loved TV growing up, but can you imagine trying to concentrate in class when Netflix is on your phone?!

Even if you've only been out of high school a few years yourself, you can probably remember how things changed, and how culture shifted so much each year while you were there. The same is true for your few—which means you'll probably still need some help understanding their world.

So while it may not always be easy to connect with the teenage girls in your small group, if you want your small group conversations to matter more, you've got to start by making a weekly connection with each of your few. If you want your small group to open up, they need to feel connected to you.

Here are three ways to get started . . .

1. CONNECT BEFORE SMALL GROUP

If conversation comes easily for your small group, you probably know what it's like to look at the clock and realize small group ends in five minutes and your group is still answering the question, "How are you?"

But if chitchat isn't exactly your small group's favorite hobby, you've probably had weeks when success looked like getting your group to speak in full sentences.

If either of these situations sounds familiar to you, whether you wish your small group time was twice as long or half as short, you might have a connection problem. But don't worry. There is an easy solution.

Connect with your few *before* small group. Some girls have a lot to say to you—more things than could possibly be covered during your small group time. When you connect with those girls before small group, you give them time to share their stories before your small group conversation begins.

Other girls need some time to warm up before they open up to you. When you connect with those girls before small group, you give them time to get comfortable so they're ready to share when your small group conversation begins.

Either way, remember this:

The QUALITY of your small group conversations will reflect the QUANTITY of your connections outside group time.

So, you might want to try . . .
checking in with them during the week.
starting a group text conversation.
meeting up for coffee a few minutes before church.
greeting them at the door.
singing alongside them during worship.
sitting with them during the teaching.
walking with them to small group.

And if you do, you might just find that small talk with a teenage girl is a little different than small talk with an adult. For starters, they're not always great at it. Teenage girls have grown up in a world where many of their conversations are typed, not spoken. So if you try making small talk with one of your few and it feels awkward, that's okay. It doesn't mean they don't like you. Like an old television antenna (remember those?), small talk with a teenager can take a few tries and minor adjustments before you get a genuine connection.

Here are a few small talk tricks that have worked for us:

The common ground game. As you chat with a girl, ask questions about *everything*: her favorite movies, what's on her playlist, sports she plays, school clubs, talents, family, everything. Don't let the interaction end until you've said "me too" and found one thing the two of you have in common. Next time you see her, you'll instantly have a conversation starter.

The follow-up. Ask about something she mentioned the last time you saw her. Maybe it was a tough test or a prayer request for her mom. Before group is a great time to connect with a girl by following up on what's most important to her. Of course remembering their hopes, dreams, and prayer requests from week-to-week isn't as easy as it sounds. So, if you need a little help, keep a note on your phone or download the Lead Small app so you can keep track of your few's prayer requests and sneak a peek right before they arrive.

The helpless leader approach. No matter how good your conversation skills are, sometimes it will be painful trying to get any interaction out of one of your few. One way to get them talking is to ask for their help. Try saying something like, "I'm looking for some new music to listen to—do you have any suggestions?" or, "Do you have any gift ideas for my 16-year-old cousin's birthday?" Some of your few may even be excited to talk about new fashion trends (and which ones adults can't pull off) or how to take your personal brand to the next level on Instagram.

Making small connections early can make a big impact on your conversation later. That's why one of the best ways to master the art of group talk is to work hard at mastering the art of small talk.

Don't let the first time you connect with your few be the moment your small group conversation starts. Connect with them and make some small talk *before* small group begins.

I (Ashley) remember the moment I decided to make connecting with my few a bigger priority. One of my girls pulled me aside and asked, "Are you upset with me?" I was a little confused because I definitely wasn't upset with her! When I asked why she felt that way, she said, "Well, you said hello to everyone in our group today, but you didn't say hello to me."

Of course I hadn't ignored her on purpose! But, still, she felt ignored.

That's when I realized a student can't connect if they don't feel noticed.

From then on, I decided to try really hard to . . .
say hello to every girl, so she feels welcome.
look every girl in the eye, so she feels seen.
say every girl's name, so she feels known.

2. CONNECT WITH NEW STUDENTS

At some point, chances are someone new will join your small group. And that's a great thing! But let's be honest. It can also be a challenge to add someone new to your group. Will she feel welcome? Will your few like her? Will they have anything in common? And how do you get them to actually *talk* to one another?

If these are the questions running through *your* mind, imagine the questions running through *hers*. When you're a teenager, being the new girl can be pretty scary. That's why it's up to you to make her feel welcome, safe, liked, and celebrated.

SMALL GROUP SURVIVAL KIT: CONFETTI POPPER
Remember that survival kit we told you to pack? Here's the first thing on your list: A confetti popper. When someone new joins your group, it's your job to help them feel connected. Celebrate their first week with your group with a confetti popper! (But maybe wait until the *end* of small group.)

In other words, connect with her. Here are a few tips you might want to try . . .

Remember her name. If this doesn't seem like a big deal, it's because you've never seen the look on a teenager's face when she realizes you've forgotten her name. Next time a new student shows up for small group, here's a tip:

1. Say her name out loud.
2. Repeat it.
3. And repeat it again.

Like this: "Your name's Jayla? It's so great to meet you. Where do you go to school, Jayla?" Repeating her name will help you remember it. And it will let her know you remember it, too.

Learn about her. Most teenage girls will be hesitant to join your small group for the first time. So to help her feel comfortable, learn more about her. Ask about her school, family, and interests. No matter what's going on around you, make her feel like the most important person in the room.

Try something like this:
"Jules, what's one thing you love and one thing you hate about school?"
"Destiny, if you could do anything for an entire weekend, what would it be?"

Find common ground. As you learn about who she is, look for ways to connect her experiences with yours.

If she loves animals, tell her about your pet hedgehog.
If she plays tennis, tell her about your terrible hand-eye coordination.
And if she loves manga but you aren't exactly sure what that is, Google it.

And if you discover it's difficult to find a commonality or to get a student talking, check out the tips we talked about in the previous section. Tricks like the common ground game and the helpless leader approach can go a long way in establishing an initial connection.

When a new student joins your small group, remember, it's your job to help her feel connected. Her experience at church is impacted by her experience with you, so don't just connect with the girls you see every week. **Connect with new students, too.**

3. CONNECT DURING SMALL GROUP

No matter how hard you try to connect with each of the girls in your small group *before* small group begins, there will be weeks when you can't . . .
hug every girl.
hear every story.
catch up on every detail.

So as your small group time begins, use the first few moments to connect with the girls you couldn't connect with before small group began.

You might be tempted to dive right into your small group conversation. We get it. You've got a lot to accomplish. But when you take the time to connect with every girl, you're not wasting precious small group time. You're laying a foundation the rest of your conversation will be built on.

So when small group begins, don't rush your few into the discussion questions. **Connect with them during small group.**

Because if you want this week's small group conversation to matter more, your few need to feel connected to you. **CONNECT WITH THEM.**

2.2

If you want your small group conversations to matter more, help them

connect with each other

Connect with each other

As a small group leader, you're a big deal. You give your few a place to belong. You show them what God is like. You love them, lead them, teach them, and coach them. Without SGLs like you, small groups wouldn't work. Your few need you!

But they also need **each other.**

Because you can't go to school with your few. You're not in third period or the cafeteria or on the bus or at practice with them, but chances are at least some of your few will be in all of those places together. And they will be able to look out for each other, encourage each other, and challenge each other in a way that you, as an adult, just can't. **You may have a great conversation on Sunday, but as a group, they will face Monday together.**

If you look back at the earliest churches, what you'll see is pretty interesting. You'll see no buildings. No choir rooms. No praise bands. There were no student programs. No Sunday school classes. No fall retreats.

There was simply community. Genuine, pure, tight-knit, nothing-to-hide, kill-my-best-goat-for-you kind of community.

The church wasn't a place. The church was a group.

As an SGL, it's your job to cultivate that kind of community.

To give your few . . .
a tribe.
a safe place.
a small group.

That's why it's not enough for your few to connect with *you*.
They need to connect with *each other*, too.

Oh, but, they're teenagers. So they may need a little help
from you.

They need you to connect them with each other.

1. CONNECT THEM WITH AN ICEBREAKER

You may have spent some time before small group
connecting with each of the girls in your group. But now
that small group has started, this may be the first time this
week they've all connected with one another.

So to help them connect
and to get the conversation started,
ask an icebreaker question.

Icebreaker questions aren't meant to be too deep or
serious—their purpose is to get the conversational juices
flowing. Sometimes, you might choose to ask something
hypothetical, like . . .
- If you could go on a road trip with any celebrity, who
  would you take and where would you go?
- If you could prove the existence of any mythical crea-
  ture, what would you want it to be?
- If you could make one movie become real—and live in
  it—what movie would you choose?

For some groups, especially in high school, students may be ready to jump into conversation by talking about their weeks. You might start group with a question like . . .

- What's the funniest thing you saw or heard this week?
- What were your HIGHS and LOWS from last week?
- What made you MAD, SAD, and GLAD this week?

Something to keep in mind when leading a group of middle schoolers is that they may be nervous to share anything that makes them stand out—after all, in middle school, being different is the worst thing you can be. That's why middle schoolers will often go with a safe and boring answer, or repeat what everyone else said. So in order to get some original answers, use a totally goofy question like . . .

- Would you rather eat a cottage cheese taco or a yogurt hot dog?
- Unicorns. Real or fake? Explain your view.
- What's the most annoying sound in the world?

Asked an icebreaker question and the group's still quiet? Call for an all-skate where basically everyone answers. Or encourage them to answer the question with the girls sitting directly next to them.

 SMALL GROUP SURVIVAL KIT: ICEBREAKER QUESTIONS
Here's the next thing on your packing list. It's not easy to come up with icebreaker questions on the spot. Trust us. We know. We've tried. They're much easier to come up with when you're *not* being stared at by a group of teenage girls (and when you have access to Google). Write down a few of your favorite icebreaker questions, and stash them in your Survival Kit for later. (Or grab a few from us at leadsmall.org!)

A good icebreaker question will give your few a chance to . . .

- talk about themselves (that means no "yes" or "no" questions).
- learn something new about each other (which should be pretty easy once they start talking).
- laugh together. (So maybe ask something other than, "What's your favorite Bible verse?")

If they don't laugh together, they'll probably never feel comfortable enough to talk with each other about their questions, their doubts, or their life experiences. So help your few connect with each other. **Connect them with an icebreaker.**

2. CONNECT THEM THROUGH THEIR INTERESTS

Maybe your small group has a lot in common.
Maybe they . . .
have all the same hobbies.
laugh at all the same jokes.
like all the same ~~boys~~ music.

But probably not.

Most likely, you're probably leading a small group of girls who are all very different. In that case, it's your job to help them discover what they have in common.

Maybe they all love puppies . . . or Frappucinos . . . or makeup tutorials . . . or death metal. If you already know something they all have in common, point out that connection.

If you're not sure what they have in common, turn it into a game. Put five minutes on the clock, and challenge them to find one thing they all have in common.

And if you're pretty sure they have absolutely *nothing* in common, try watching a video of cats. Cat videos bring everyone together.

So help your few connect with each other. **Connect them through their interests.** (And cat videos.)

3. CONNECT THEM WITH SOMEONE NEW

It's not always easy for teenage girls to connect with someone new. Even inside your small group, you've probably noticed that some girls don't connect quite as well as others. And that's okay. You can't force your girls to be friends, but you can encourage them to make a new connection.

If you are a high school small group leader you might want to try . . .
splitting into pairs to answer an icebreaker question.
splitting into *new* pairs for the next question.
splitting into even more new pairs until everyone has had a chance to connect with someone new.

But even though splitting into pairs can be a big win in high school groups, if you're a middle school SGL, you may notice pair-and-share can sometimes be uncomfortable for new students. Instead, you might choose to have students talk in groups of three, to alleviate the pressure of carrying on conversation with someone they don't know yet. Or try making teams and playing some sort of game or having a competition. That way it's not forcing them to have a conversation, but doing something together in order to connect.

Or you could just say . . .
"Hey Priya! Did you know Jess runs track too?"

I (Crystal) remember leading a group with a girl named Sydney who just love Korean pop music. Each week, she would make me a playlist, I'd listen, and we'd talk about the oh-so-good-looking K-pop star of the week. A few months in, a new girl named Kate visited our group. When I asked what kind of music she liked, Kate responded, "I love K-pop." At that exact moment, angels began to sing and lights shone down from heaven. Okay, not really. But it was super fun to introduce the two girls, and explain what they had in common. Kate and Sydney couldn't have been more different. They never became best friends, but when they saw each other in group, they instantly had something to talk about.

Whatever this looks like for you, give it a try this week. Help your few connect with each other. **Connect them with someone new.**

And remember, if you want your small group conversations to matter more, you might want to try this before the conversation begins: **connect with them and help them connect with each other.**

Because before a teenager can connect with *God*, she may need to connect with *someone* who's connected with God.

QUIZ:

HOW WELL DO YOU CONNECT WITH YOUR FEW?

Group time has started, and it's up to you to get the conversation going in a direction that invites everyone in! Before you can go deeper, it's probably a good idea to connect with your few. Answer the questions below to see how well you CONNECT with your few each week.

What's the best way you've found to check in with your few during the week?

Do you show up early enough to connect with each of your girls before small group begins?

QUIZ

Do the girls in your group usually connect with each other before small group begins?

What's your go-to icebreaker question?
(You know, other than, "How was your week?")

What was the last thing that made your whole group laugh? Like really hard?

QUIZ

If we picked a random name from your small group roster, could you tell us three things about her?

✎

When a new girl joins or visits your group, how do you help her feel comfortable and connected?

✎

NEXT STEP

We know the art of CONNECTION looks different for everyone. Below, write one or two specific and practical things you can do to better CONNECT with your few before group this week.

3

chapter three
know

Know

(Talk about YOURSELVES)

So let's say you've . . .
prepared for your small group conversation.
connected with your few.
and helped your few connect with each other.

Now—*finally*—you can start having a conversation about faith.

Right?

Well . . .
Almost.
Hang in there for just a few more minutes.

There's one more thing you should probably do before you have a conversation with your few about faith.

But first, imagine this.

You're face-to-face with someone you barely know and they ask, "So what spiritual battle are you facing right now?" or, "How are you practicing sexual integrity?" or, "Is there somewhere in your life you need to repent?"

Um . . . awkward, right?

Of course it is! Because we don't have personal, meaningful, and authentic conversations with people unless we have relationships with them that are personal, meaningful, and authentic.

Think about it.
Who was the last person you had an
honest
open
meaningful
conversation with?

It probably wasn't a stranger or a random acquaintance.
More than likely, it was your best friend, your mom, your
spouse, or a mentor. You know—someone you trust.
Someone who loves you. Someone who *knows* you.

Teenage girls are no different. They want to have honest
conversations about things that matter—like faith, for
example. But they want to have those conversations with
the *right* people.

Teenage girls won't have honest conversations with
just *anyone.*
But they will have them with safe people.
They won't have honest conversations *anytime*
or anywhere.
But they will have them in safe places.

So if you want to have better small group conversations,
make sure your small group feels like a safe place. And
if you want your small group to feel like a safe place,
make sure your small group conversations don't feel like
conversations with strangers. Make sure your small group is
a place where your few feel *known.*

But here's the thing about being known.
(It might sound obvious, but stay with us.)

A teenage girl won't *feel* known until someone *knows* her.
If you want the girls in your group to feel known,
you can't force it
and you can't fake it.

The only way to help a teenager feel known
is to **actually know her.**

That's why, as an SGL, it's your job to
know the girls in your group
and help them *know* each other.

Knowing—really knowing—your small group is a big deal.

Because **before a teenage girl can KNOW *God* loves her,
she may need to be KNOWN by *people* who know God.**

3.1

If you want your small group
conversations to
matter more,

know
them

Know them

It's not enough just to **connect** with the girls in your group. You've got to really **know** them—and I don't just mean your favorites. If you want your small group conversations to matter more, you've got to know every girl.

So, before you lead a conversation with teenage girls, there are a few things you need to know about teenagers. First, it's great to recognize where they're at developmentally. This means understanding the phase they're in and all that comes with it emotionally, physically, and socially. *

To get you started, here are some summaries of what girls may be experiencing in each grade (of course, these might not be true of ALL middle and high school girls, but they do apply to MANY of them):

For **sixth-grade** girls, life is all about figuring out who they like—and who likes them. Your girls will likely become obsessed with peer approval, yet be totally unaware of it. They'll go to great lengths to fit in. Friendships change, hormones kick in, and their interests shift. This means creating a safe place in your small group is essential so they have a place they can stop attempting to fit in, and just be themselves.

---

* If you're looking for great resources about the developmental changes students experience from year to year, check out justaphase.com. It's full of resources for parents and leaders just like you—helping you make the most of every phase.

Seventh grade is the year of personal discovery. They'll try things they have never tried before. Not everyone will make the team. Everything about themselves is changing. And everything is done en masse. They walk the hall in pairs. They go to the mall in a herd. They build unfathomably large social media platforms. Planning group outings with your girls will be one of the best ways to connect with them, and help them connect with each other.

Eighth graders are beginning to think about who they want to become one day. They realize they don't have to believe what they have been told to believe, and they don't have to behave how they have been told to behave. They'll doubt, question, and debate. They want to make their own decisions. So, help them sort through the options.

Ninth grade is all about finding a group of friends where you fit. Girls may talk a lot about finding or changing friend groups. That means spending extra time connecting is a good idea. And connecting outside group with girls who feel lonely or left out is essential.

Tenth grade is the time when students begin to question everything. Don't panic if your sweet ninth graders are now challenging everything you've taught them. That's normal. Instead, make group conversations a safe place to ask questions and express doubt.

Eleventh grade is when students start driving, working, and dating. That means you may see a drop in small group attendance, but don't let that be where the conversation ends. Stay in touch with girls who seem to have checked out, letting them know it's always okay to check back in.

Twelfth-grade girls tend to have equal parts excitement and anxiety about what this last year means for them. This is the time to begin helping them see community is about the people, not the building or the small group itself.

So spend time with girls outside group, helping them to connect relationally so they'll still have those friendships when they leave.

Once you understand some of what's happening developmentally in the lives of your few, if you want your small group conversations to matter more, you need to know every girl personally.

When you know a teenage girl personally, you know . . .
her name.
her birthday.
her family.
her talents.
her fears.
her hopes.
her food allergies.

When you know her, you know about . . .
her week.
her friends.
her exam on Monday.
her game on Friday.
her new crush.
her fight with her mom.
her new shoes that are just "ah-mazing."

Maybe that seems like a lot of things to know about every girl in your group.
We're not saying you need to know
everything that happens
every week
to every girl.
Especially if you have 19 girls and counting on your roster.
We're just saying if you want your few to feel known in your small group, you're going to need to know them.

Here are a few ways to KNOW your few . . .

1. KNOW THEIR WORLDS

Remember when we talked about how to PREPARE for your small group conversation? One of the ways we suggested preparing for your conversation was to **consider what's happening in their lives right now.**

It makes sense, right? There are certain things that would be helpful to know before small group begins.

Before you ask what they're doing this weekend, it would be nice to know Friday is Maria's birthday.

Before you begin a discussion about gossip, you might want to know about the rumor Jasmine started about Elsa this week.

Before you lead a conversation about trusting God as a heavenly Father, you should probably know that Lincoln's dad just left.

If you want to get to know a student's world, it helps to . . .

1.   Show up in her world. No matter how much your few tell you about their school, it doesn't compare to seeing it for yourself. So go visit a high school basketball game. Bring donuts to the parking lot before class and meet some of their friends. If your girls don't drive yet, offer to pick a few of your girls up from cheer practice and show up a little early. I (Crystal) signed up to substitute teach once each semester because understanding a high schooler's world means spending time around real teenagers *outside* a church.

2.   Know her family. A middle schooler is beginning to gain her independent identity, but she is still very much a product of her family. The family schedule, plans, friends, and vacations revolve around what the

guardian decides. Middle schoolers don't always get to choose which parent they want to stay with. They can't just make plans and go without parental permission. Their plans are made for them most of the time. So walk her out to the car after group to get a minute with her parent, follow her parents on social media, organize an event that parents can come to, ask the student questions about family traditions, dynamics, and plans. You can tell a lot about a student's world when you know her family, because her family is still so much of her world.

3. Engage with her on social media. Instagram is like a cheat sheet to see a snippet of your girls' daily lives. And bonus points if they let you follow their fake or spam account too. Some girls have those, not because they want to post anything scandalous, but because they need a place to post when they're feeling silly or angry or no-makeup-dying-laughing. When you follow your girls on social media, you get to see the world the way they see it.

4. Follow who she follows. Most of your few aren't subscribing to magazines or listening to radio stations. The people and bands and companies influencing their worldviews are the ones they follow on social media. So it helps if you follow them too. Do most of your few follow a particular Spotify playlist? Try to listen to it once or twice a week. Do some of them follow a group of celebrities or a TV channel's social media account? Subscribe. We get it. A teen fashion magazine's Instagram story may not be your cup of tea, but it helps to know what words, images, and ideas feel normal to your few. It gives context to your conversation. So follow who they follow. And if you're not sure, ask them!

It was during a teaching series on healthy relationship that I (Ashley) learned firsthand the value of knowing a student's world. Before small group, one of my few told me her boyfriend had cheated on her—but she was furious with the other girl, not her boyfriend. Having this knowledge in advance made a big difference in how I prepared for our small group discussion that week. I knew it would be important to spend more time talking about healthy qualities and characteristics in relationships so she would be able to connect the dots.

The more you know about a teenager's world before your small group conversation begins, the better your conversation will be. When you know what's happening in their world, you'll be more likely to know . . .
what to say.
what not to say.
when to celebrate them.
when to challenge them.
when to comfort them.

SMALL GROUP SURVIVAL KIT: NOISEMAKER

When you know your few, you know when they need to be celebrated. But it's not exactly easy to keep track of everything that's happening in their lives. That's why it's helpful to keep a noisemaker on hand. Because whether it's because of a birthday, a report card, a great game, or a new record time in Mario Kart, sometimes one of your few will need to be celebrated—and you'll need to be prepared.

You don't need to know *everything* about your girls' lives before you begin a small group conversation. The truth is that a good small group conversation will probably teach you something new about your few. But you shouldn't have to wait for small group time to catch up on their lives.

So don't.

If you want to know about their worlds . . .
follow them on social media.
text them during the week.
ask how they're doing.
follow up on their prayer requests.
talk with their parents.

If you want your small group conversations to matter more, it's not enough for you to simply **CONNECT** with your few each week. You've got to **KNOW** them—really know them. And you can start by **knowing their worlds.**

2. KNOW THEIR PERSONALITIES

This might be a wild guess.
We could be completely wrong.

But we're going to assume that your small group is filled with a few different types of personalities.

We're also going to assume that managing those personalities can sometimes be a challenge. Especially when you're trying to lead a small group conversation.

Some girls dominate the conversation
while others never say a word.

Some are silly
and some are serious.

Some are outgoing
and some are reserved.

Some will follow the group
while some will try to lead it.

Some are self-aware
and some are completely oblivious.

It won't always be easy to have a conversation with so many competing personalities, but here are a few tips that might help:

Know Your Extroverts They have a lot to say. They enjoy being the center of attention. On a good day, the extroverts in your group probably fill the room with energy, keep the conversation moving, and get everyone laughing. But on a bad day, they leave you with ringing ears, a hoarse voice, and a desperate need for a nap. No matter what kind of day you have this week with your few, here are a few tips for leading an extroverted teenage girl in a small group conversation.

Be patient with them. Remember, your few are not adults—they're teenage girls. They're still learning to be self-aware and emotionally intelligent. In the meantime, if they're too loud, if they interrupt too often or if they've been talking for longer than you'd like, be patient. When you correct them, correct them with kindness (and maybe even a little humor). And remember, if you treat your extroverts with patience, grace, and dignity, they'll be much more likely to use their energy and words for the good of your conversation next time.

Hear them. After they've said what must be their 500,000th word of the day, it's not easy to give your extroverts your full attention. But keep this in mind: They still deserve your focused attention. And once they feel heard, they'll be more likely to focus and less likely to try to dominate the conversation.

Empower them. I (Crystal) remember doing an in-town weekend retreat with my group. A few were introverts. A few were extroverts. And about three of them? They were more like zoo animals. They were loud and crazy. They weren't disrespectful, but on a scale of 1-10, their energy level was at 11 all day every day. I remember driving them toward our free time activity as they danced so violently that my car was shaking. So just before we arrived, I turned off the stereo and said, "Hey. We need to chat." They immediately responded "Oh. We're sorry. Are we too loud?" "Not at all!" I responded. "I actually want you to keep being loud. You see we're about to walk into free time, and it could be awesome or it could be a total flop. The difference will be the energy you guys bring. You're party-starters and I want you to bring the party to this free-time activity. Cool?" They were bought in. In fact, everywhere we went that weekend I would ask "Hey, can you guys be party-starters when we get there?" They made the weekend more fun for everyone and felt like they were part of leading the group.

You see, that's the great thing about having extroverts—especially when you're an introverted leader.
They bring the energy so you don't have to create it.
They start the party so you don't always have to.

SMALL GROUP SURVIVAL KIT: STRESS BALL
Have you ever led a conversation where *everyone* had something to say? About everything? At the exact same time? In those moments, you need a stress ball (and maybe some ear plugs). Here's how to use it—you know, besides the obvious way:

1. Clear your throat dramatically.
2. Say, "For the rest of small group, you may only speak if you're holding this ball."
3. Give the ball to the teenager of your choice. If they follow your instructions, invest $5.00 and buy cupcakes next week as a reward.

Know Your Introverts They're quiet. They're reserved. They sometimes observe your conversations more than they participate (especially if you have a handful of them in your group). Your introverts probably aren't the first to respond to a small group question, but when you can get them to speak, you're usually glad they did. A small group conversation can be an intimidating environment for an introvert, so here are a few tips for keeping them involved in the conversation . . .

Don't forget them. It's pretty easy to favor your extroverts during a small group conversation. It makes sense. They're always ready to answer. But don't forget about your introverts! They may not be as vocal during your small group conversation, but that's not because they're not engaged in it. In fact, they're probably thinking deeply about the conversation. So in your next small group conversation, don't forget to engage your introverts. They have a lot to contribute.

Don't surprise them. Introverts don't usually like to be put on the spot. There are few things more uncomfortable for an introverted teenage girl than being asked to speak in front of a group unexpectedly. So if you want them to participate, give them a heads up. Say something like, "Hey Caprice, after this, you've got the next question." Or try, "I'd love to hear what you think about this in a second, but let me tell you a story first." You might even want to try slipping them the questions in advance so they can think about their responses before the conversation begins.

Don't force them. As you get to know your introverts, you'll begin to learn when to push them to speak and when to let them sit back and observe. As an SGL, you'll figure out when to challenge your few without making them feel pressured, uncomfortable, or embarrassed.

It's not easy to lead a group filled with competing personalities, but you can do it! The more you get to know your few, the better you'll be at managing the conversation.

If you want to make your small group conversations matter more, you'll need to **KNOW** your few. And you can do that by **knowing their personalities.**

SMALL GROUP SURVIVAL KIT:
DECK OF CARDS

Sometimes you need to shift the balance of power between your talkers and non-talkers. A great tip we got from a fellow SGL was to always bring a deck of cards to group—regular cards, *Uno* cards, *Candy Land* cards—any cards will work. Hand them out at the beginning of your group time, and when it comes to answering questions you can call on all the "blues" or all of the "6s" to answer the next question. Now you've got a reason to let everyone have an equal chance at sharing during group!

3. KNOW THEIR DISTRACTIONS

If you've ever led a group of teenagers, you know that keeping their attention feels a lot like playing whack-a-mole. Every time you squash one distraction, another pops up. (However, we don't recommend hitting your students with mallets. Please don't do that.)

Here are just a few examples of distractions that might pop up for middle schoolers:
- Poking each other
- Needing to go to the bathroom
- Wanting to accompany their friend to the bathroom
- Hearing other small groups talking or laughing
- Knowing they're going to get donuts after small group

Common distractions for high schoolers may look more like this:
- Something dramatic happened before group
- Figuring out the plan for what's happening after group

- A rumor at school
- Texts and notifications
- Boys. Boys. Boys.

 SMALL GROUP SURVIVAL KIT: ZIPPER STORAGE BAG
There are few things more distracting during a small group conversation than a phone. If you've ever had to pause a conversation because someone was texting, posting, direct messaging, talking, or filming, you might want to keep a large zipper storage bag handy. On the weeks you don't want to fight a battle against their phones, start your small group by asking everyone (including you) to drop their phones into the bag until the conversation is over.

I don't know what the distractions are for your small group. Maybe it's braiding each other's hair.
Or being on their phones.
Or whispering about a group of boys.
Or everyone taking fifteen separate trips to the bathroom.

Whatever it is for your small group, you might want to pay attention to the things that distract your few from your small group conversation because when you know what distracts them, you can help eliminate those distractions *before* they derail your conversation.

If you want to make your small group conversations matter more, you'll need to **KNOW** your few. When you know their worlds, know their personalities and know their distractions, you'll be better equipped to lead your small group conversations.

Because if you want this week's small group conversation to matter more, your few need to feel known by you. **KNOW THEM**.

3.2

If you want your small group conversations to matter more, help them

know each other

Know each other

You already know how important it is for you to know your few. But just like how you need to help your few connect with each other, you're not the only person your few need to be *known* by. They need to know, and be known by, each other.

We've already said that before a teenage girl can KNOW *God* loves her, she may need to be KNOWN by *people* who know God. But if you're still not convinced that helping your few get to know each other will significantly impact their faith, then consider this.

Just like the people in ancient times developed their view of God as . . .
the God of Abraham,
the God of Isaac,
or the God of Moses,

you have developed a sense of who God is because you have met . . .
the God of Talicia,
the God of Amanda,
or the God of Janet.

Here's the point. God has always used people to demonstrate His story of redemption.

It was true then. And it's true today.
It was true for you. And it's true for your few.

So if you want a teenage girl to know God, maybe one of the most important things you can do is to give her a community of people who will talk with her, hang out with her, and do life with her. People who know God and who know her.

You're one of those people.
But you're not the only person she needs.
She needs to know (and be known by) you.
But she needs to know (and be known by) the rest of her small group too.

So make sure you know your few. Then help them know each other.

Here are a few ways to do that . . .

1. MAKE GROUP MEMORIES

Nothing creates a connection like a shared memory.

If you want to move your few
from casually **connecting** with each other
to really **knowing** each other,
you might want to consider making some
memories together.

When you make memories together *outside* of small group, instead of only seeing each other *inside* of small group, you'll help your few know each other better. And when they know one another better, they'll have better conversations.

Cook a meal together.
Go apple-picking.
Ride a roller coaster.
Sing really loud to their favorite song.

Camp out.
Go on a road trip.
Cheer one of the girls on in her big game.
Throw a surprise party.

When you're back together *inside* of small group, take time to talk about the memories you made *outside* of small group. And then make plans to make some new ones. It'll help your few know each other. And it will help them grow together. When you're building new relationships, shared memories are like the cement. You'll need lots of them, but it'll make your foundation strong. So **make group memories** together.

2. BUILD GROUP IDENTITY

We are all created for community.
We all want a place to belong.
We all long to be part of . . .
A group.
A family.
A tribe.

We all want to know *these people* are *our people*.

If you don't believe me, go to a football game. Check out the team colors. The face paint. The screaming. Now *those* people are passionate about their tribes.

Your few are no different. Okay, they probably don't paint their faces and scream during small group (or maybe they do), but it's still true. The girls in your small group want a place to belong. They want a tribe, a family, and a group that they can call their own.

If you want your small group to really know each other, you might want to help them see themselves as a group by building a stronger group identity.

How? Well, you could try . . .
starting a group text.
planning a small group hangout.
making matching T-shirts.
sitting together during the service.
inventing a new small group tradition.
having an inside joke.

Because when your group has a strong sense of group
identity, they'll feel like a tribe, a family, and a group.
They'll feel like they belong. And when they feel like they
belong, they'll be more likely to open up. So help your few
know each other. **Build group identity together.**

3. SET GROUP GUIDELINES

If you want your few to *know* each other, making memories
and building group identity will help. But if you want
your few to *really* know each other, they need to feel safe
enough to
be . . .
real.
vulnerable.
honest.

That's where confidentiality comes in.

But since you're a small group leader, you probably know
that confidentiality isn't exactly easy to monitor. You
typically won't know about a breach until after . . .
Sawyer has told the whole volleyball team what Sadie said
about them in group.
Tiffany has tweeted about Gabriela's disgusting
foot fungus.
Tia has shown the whole class pictures of Tamera's ugly cry
at church camp.

We would all love to have the perfect group filled with
enough respect and maturity to know for sure that what is

said in group stays in group. In fact, that should probably
be a rule you set up in the beginning. Absolute, 100
percent, swear-on-my-brand-new-iPhone confidentiality
should always be your goal. But as the grown ups, we have
to be realistic.

You probably won't be able to prevent every breach in
confidentiality, but you can challenge your few to set
guidelines that will help your small group feel safe.

And since they're teenagers, it's probably a good idea to
let them be part of the guideline setting process. When
they're part of the process of setting group guidelines,
they'll be more likely to feel responsible for
maintaining them.

So set some group guidelines. Together.
You might want to start by asking them . . .
What will our group *always* do?
What will our group *never* do?
How will we treat each other?

The thing with high school girls is they may answer these
questions with exactly what you're looking for. You don't
have to sell them on the *idea* of having group guidelines.
The challenge is selling them on actually following them.

I (Crystal) have found it helpful not only to remind girls
what our group guidelines are, but why we have them in
the first place. The conversation sometimes goes like this:

Me: So what happens if someone breaks confidentiality in
our group?
Girls: We kill them!
Me: Um, no. Seriously. What would *really* happen?
Girls: No one shares anymore.
Me: Sort of. People will probably still talk since 30 minutes
of silence is weird.
Girls: No one would share anything real. We'd all just give

easy answers and be . . . well, fake.

Me: Exactly. So the real question isn't, "Will we protect confidentiality?" The real question is, "Do we want to come to a group every week where people are real or where people are fake?"

This reveals that when you set group guidelines, your few will be much more likely to feel safe enough to be honest in your small group conversations. And honesty is a crucial part of getting to know each other. Help your few know each other. **Set group guidelines** together. And remind your few of them often.

Note on confidentiality: As a small group leader, your few might open up to you about some serious stuff. If one of your few shares something that qualifies as one of the three hurts—hurting themselves, hurting others, or being hurt by another—you should talk to your church staff.

If you want your small group conversations to matter more, you might want to make this part of your weekly conversation: **know them and help them know each other.**

Because before a teenager can know *God,* she may need to be known by *someone* who knows God.

QUIZ:

HOW WELL DO YOU KNOW YOUR FEW?

Energy drink or latte? Sports or band? Dance or tae kwon do? Answer the questions below to see how well you KNOW your few.

How well do your few know each other? Do they know each other's . . . (circle yes or no)

Names?   **Birthdays?**

Yes   No   Yes   No

Crushes?   **Pet Peeves?**

Yes   No   Yes   No

Which of your few do you know the least?
(Write her name here and set a reminder in your phone to connect with her outside group some time this week.)

QUIZ

List two or three of your favorite small group memories.

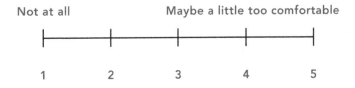

_____

_____

_____

_____

_____

_____

_____

How comfortable are your few with being open and honest during your small group conversations? (circle one)

Not at all   Maybe a little too comfortable

|———————|———————|———————|———————|

1   2   3   4   5

NEXT STEP

We know the art of knowing your group looks a little different for everyone. Below, write one or two specific and practical things you can do to get to KNOW your few even better this week.

NEXT STEP

4

chapter four
engage

Engage

(Talk about the TRUTH)

Okay.
Finally.
This is the part you've been waiting for.

Now that you've
prepared for your small group conversation,
connected as a group,
and gotten to **know** each other,
you're ready to actually **engage** your small group
in a conversation.

But not just any conversation.
A really important conversation.
A conversation about authentic faith.

After all, that's why you became an SGL in the first place,
isn't it? So you could lead teenagers in conversations about
truths that will shape their faith and future.

Sure, it's taken us some time to get here, but that was
intentional. Before we could talk about building authentic
faith in your small group, we had to talk about building
authentic relationships first.

When you take the time to invest relationally in your
few by . . .
connecting with them
helping them connect with each other
knowing them
helping them know each other

. . . you lay a foundation of trust, influence and relationships that you're going to need if you want your few to ultimately engage in a conversation about faith.

But before we go any further, let's clarify something.

Let's talk about that word **ENGAGE.**

Maybe we could have called this chapter **TALK.**
Or **DISCUSS.**
Or **PARTICIPATE.**
Although talking, discussing, and participating are *some* of the things you probably hope your small group will do, those words don't quite capture the goal of a small group conversation. Not completely.

You see, when you're finally ready to begin a conversation about authentic faith with your small group, your goal isn't for them to simply talk, discuss, or *participate* in your conversation.

When your few participate in a conversation, they might . . .
listen.
respond.
be respectful.
summarize.

But when they *engage* in a conversation, they'll do more than participate. They will . . .
think.
share.
question.
discuss.
debate.
own.
personalize.

In fact, as former teachers, we experienced the value of engagement all the time. When we asked students to simply recall or summarize what they learned, they would soon forget it. But when we crafted lessons around debating, discussing, and personalizing—in other words, *engaging*— with each other, the students were always more likely to remember it down the road. And even though your role as an SGL isn't supposed to look like that of a classroom teacher, engaging your few in a conversation will go a long way in making the conversation stick. And that's what we want, right?

But with teenage girls, engagement can be tricky—at least, when you're talking about faith. If you're discussing Taylor Swift or puppies, engaging teenage girls in a conversation is simple. But when you're not talking about T-Swift or puppies—when you're talking about doubt or forgiveness or prayer or sexual integrity—how do you move your few beyond simply *participating* in the conversation?

How do you **ENGAGE** them in a conversation about authentic faith?

Learning to engage your few in your conversations won't always be easy. You won't always get it right. It won't always come naturally. But no matter how your small group conversation went *last* week, there is always something you can do to better engage your few *next* week.

So if you want to better engage your few in your small group conversations, there are a few things you'll probably need to do *less*. You may need to . . .
talk less.
control less.
script less.

And there are a few things you'll probably need to do *more*. Like . . .
listen more.
lead more.
improvise more.

As you work to better engage your few in conversations about faith, there will still be weeks when you'll feel frustrated. There will still be weeks when you'll wish you'd said or done or handled things differently. There will still be weeks you'll wonder if you're really cut out for this small-group-leading thing.

We know. We've been there.

Leading a small group can be difficult. And trying to engage a group of teenage girls in a conversation about authentic faith might be the most difficult part. (That and trying to keep up with both their real and fake social media accounts.)

So on the weeks when it's difficult to engage your few in a faith conversation, it wouldn't hurt to remember this.

Your few won't remember every small group conversation you'll ever have.
But they will remember more than you think.

Even on the weeks when you're sure they weren't engaged in your conversation, **what gets said in small group probably has more of an impact than you think it does.** The words your few share in small group may seem like small things, but they have tremendous influence.

Remember what we said earlier? **Your small group conversations matter**—maybe more than you think. But with the right amount of preparation, relationships, technique, and patience, **you can make your small group conversations matter even more.**

So if you want to make your small group conversations matter more (and we know you do), then you might want to be more intentional about how you engage your few during your conversations about faith.

Because before a teenage girl can ENGAGE in a life of authentic faith, she may need you to ENGAGE her in a conversation about authentic faith.

And here are three ways to do just that.

4.1

If you want your small group conversations to matter more,

speak less, listen more.

(Let's talk about you.)

speak less, listen more

We may not know you, but if you're leading a small group of teenage girls, we're going to guess you took this job because . . .
you love God.
you love teenagers.
you want to tell teenagers about God.

No matter the reason, you signed up to help teenagers get to know God better, and that's awesome.

But trying to *tell* teenagers everything you know about God probably isn't the most effective way to influence their faith. If simply *telling* teenagers what to believe led to a more authentic faith, we wouldn't even need small groups. We could just preach longer sermons.

You know better, though.
You know the power of a small group.
You know the importance of a community.
And you know the impact you can have on a teenager's faith through conversation.

Teachers know this too. That's why they assign group projects, give lab partners, have class discussions, and encourage classroom debates. Teachers understand that teenagers learn better in environments that are collaborative and conversational than they do in lectures. Maybe that's because of how teenagers' brains are

developing during this phase.
Or because they're learning to understand multiple points
of view.
Or because they tend to trust their peers more than they
trust adults.
Or because they're occasionally skeptical of
authority figures.
Or because they often process ideas better when they talk
about them out loud.

Or maybe it's because of all these things.

Whatever the reasons, it's true. Whether the topic is
algebra, chemistry, or the Great Commandment, teenagers
learn best when they can . . .
talk about it.
ask questions.
share their opinions.
find answers together.
teach someone else.

But sometimes SGLs forget about that.
Sometimes *we* want to be the person who . . .
talks about it.
asks the questions.
shares our opinions.
has all the answers.

If you want your small group conversations to matter,
you have to let them be conversations and not just
lessons. Because, you see, you're not a teacher. You're
a small group leader. And as an SGL, you'll need to talk
sometimes. But more importantly, you'll need to listen.

In fact, we recommend sticking with the 80/20 Rule. In
every small group conversation, you should spend at least
80 percent of your time *listening,* and only 20 percent of
your time *talking.*

That's what we mean by **speaking less and listening more.**

Okay, we know. The 80/20 Rule might seem unrealistic. Depending on the particular group of teenagers you lead, maybe it is. If that's the case, make it the 60/40 Rule! The principle is still the same: speak less, and listen more.

But here's the thing. Even when we *try* to be better listeners, we're usually not very good at it. In fact, when one of your few is speaking, you will probably only pay attention to 48 percent of what she says. And of the 48 percent that you hear, you'll only remember 50 percent of it. *(These numbers are entirely made up, but we're pretty sure they're accurate.)* But don't feel too bad about it. It's not just you. We're all far worse at listening than we probably think we are.

But if you want to engage your few in a better small group conversation, you'll need to become a better conversationalist. And that starts with being a good listener. Being a good listener takes practice. So here are four steps you can take to **speak less and listen more.**

1. LOOK

Now, this might sound obvious, but stick with us. When one of the girls in your small group is speaking,
look at her.

(We told you it might sound obvious.)

But if we're honest, we'd probably all agree that making eye contact during a conversation isn't always easy or natural.

Especially when there are so many interesting things happening on your phone.
Or when you can't remember which question you're supposed to ask next.
Or when the girls to your left are discussing their plans for

the weekend in what they probably think are whispers, but are definitely not whispers.

Making eye contact with your few isn't always easy (especially in a small group setting), but it's a big deal.

However, if you find yourself frustrated that a student won't make eye contact with you while you're talking, consider the fact that maybe they're shy, or that maybe in their culture, a way of showing respect is to look down and not look a person in the eyes. That's okay because you can look at them when they speak, even if they're not looking back at you.

When you look at your few as they speak, you communicate that what they say matters. And if they believe what they say matters, they'll be a lot more likely to keep talking. So put the phone down, ignore the window, even ignore the rest of your group for just a minute, and **look when they're speaking.**

2. FOCUS

Looking at your few when they're talking is a great step toward becoming a better listener, but it's only the first step. If a girl in your group is talking and you're busy . . . rehearsing what you'll say next
wondering if you could pull off her shade of eyeshadow
thinking about your plans for after group
. . . then it doesn't matter how well you've maintained eye contact. Your listening skills still need some work.

We have a friend named Heather. Heather is a middle school pastor in Minnesota, and she's one of the best listeners we know. That's why when Heather told us she had a trick for becoming a better listener, we knew we had to . . . well, listen. Heather said that when a teenage girl is speaking, asking a question, or telling a story, she imagines she's wearing a set of blinders. (When Heather told us this, she actually put her hands on either side of her face, just in case we didn't get the picture.) She told us that those imaginary blinders are a reminder to stay focused on the girl in front of her no matter what. Even if someone tries to interrupt or her phone vibrates or she gets hit in the back of the head with a dodgeball, Heather is committed to staying focused on the girl in front of her.

The second step to becoming a better listener is to **focus on what your few are saying.**

3. SUMMARIZE

Once you've mastered the art of looking and focusing while one of the girls in your group is speaking, it's time to take your listening skills one step further. Once you've heard what she's said, take a second to **summarize what you heard.**

We've already said that we're not always the best listeners. But teenage girls aren't exactly the best communicators either. They can be . . .
long-winded.
hasty.
negative.
off-track.

(Okay, let's face it—so can we.) Your teenage girls might even tell stories so long that, when it ends, no one can remember why the story was being told in the first place. That's why summarizing is so important. When you summarize what your few have said, you help the conversation move forward.

You might say something like . . .
"So to summarize, _____ ."
"In other words, _____ ."
"So you're saying, _____ ."
"You're telling me _____ ."

When you summarize what you've heard, you . . .
let them know you're listening.
make sure you understand.
help clarify their thoughts for the rest of the group.
lead the conversation.

4. ASK

After you've summarized what one of your few has said, don't move on until you've **asked** her this question: "Did I get that right?" Because the reality is no matter how great you are at listening to a teenage girl, you will sometimes misunderstand what she's trying to say.

So when you've summarized what she said, ask if you understood her. There are two ways she could respond.

1. She could correct you. If she does, that's great! It means you're getting clarity.

2. She could agree with you. Cue the confetti. Your girl feels heard, known, understood and is now more likely to engage in conversation in the future.

But just a word of caution: It could also mean she feels uncomfortable correcting you. That's why knowing your few is so important. The more you know them, the more likely you'll be able to discern when they're being open and when they're holding back.

So before you move on to the next question, **ask if you understood her.**

If you want to make your small group conversations matter more, you'll need to **ENGAGE** your few in those conversations. And this starts with becoming a better listener. So when your few open up, don't forget to look, focus, summarize, and ask. That's what it means to **speak less and listen more.**

QUIZ:

HOW WELL DO YOU LISTEN TO YOUR FEW?

Have you ever heard of active listening? It's a GREAT tool for small group leaders. The basic idea is that you are ENGAGED as someone is telling you a story or something about themselves. Here are a few questions you should ask yourself to see if you're a good listener.

When someone in your group is talking, how often do you try to finish her sentences? (circle one)

Not often   All the time   Only with the eternal talker

When you're telling a story, what are some signs your few have definitely stopped listening? (draw or write them here)

QUIZ

When one of your few is telling a story, what are some things that make it difficult to stay focused?

What percent of your small group conversation do you usually spend speaking? (pick an actual number)

NEXT STEP

We know the art of LISTENING looks different for
everyone. Below, write one or two specific and practical
things you can do to better LISTEN to your few this
week (even the one whose story from last week made
you pray for the fire alarm to go off).

NEXT STEP

4.2

If you want your small group conversations to matter more,

control less, lead more.

(Let's talk about your questions.)

control less, lead more

When you're preparing to lead a small group conversation, it's a good idea to **think with the end in mind.** Thinking with the end in mind means deciding where you want your small group conversation to go. When you identify a destination before your conversation begins, you'll be a lot more likely to actually get there.

After all, you're the small group leader. So if you're going to lead a conversation with your few, you should have an idea of where you're leading them.

So what's your destination exactly? Well, this changes every week.

If your student pastor sends you a weekly update through email or an app, your destination might already be determined for you. To find out, open your weekly communication (if you've got one), and look for a summary of that week's conversation. If you're really lucky, your student pastor may have even summarized the topic into a catchy bottom line like . . .
Remember God is with you.
Make the wise choice.
Be the friend you want to have.

That summary, or bottom line, is your student pastor's destination. It's what they'll be teaching. It's the one idea they hope the teenagers in your ministry will learn and remember all week long.

But that's not *your* destination.
Well . . . okay, it's *almost* your destination.
But not exactly.

You see, if you were **teaching** teenagers, your destination
would be to help them **learn** or **remember** what
you've taught.

But you're not a teacher. You're a small group leader. So
your destination isn't *just* to help them learn or remember
what they've heard from your student pastor. Your
destination is to help your few **personalize** and **apply** what
they've heard.

Let's say your student pastor is teaching, "Make the
wise choice." Then your destination for your small
group conversation might be to help each of your
students identify one thing they can do to start making
wiser choices.

If your student pastor is teaching, "Remember God is with
you," your destination might be to challenge your few to
consider how their lives might be different if they really
believed God was with them.

See the difference?

In large group, the destination is **knowledge.**
In small group, the destination is **application.**

So you've got your destination in mind. Great.
Now you just have to get your group from where they are
to where you want them to go.

Easy, right?

(If you answered yes, we're not convinced you've ever met
a teenage girl before. The only place it's easy to get a
teenage girl to go is Forever 21.)

So how do you get your few to your destination? We're so glad you asked!

You have two options.
You can control them (or at least try).
Or you can lead them somewhere.

Some SGLs make the mistake of trying to control their small group conversations. They know where they're going. They know how to get there. They have a map. They have a schedule. They're going to make sure their few get to their destination *no matter what*. And they're definitely not going to sightsee or stop for Doritos® on the way.

That approach is probably helpful if you're trying to get your mission team to their flight on time, but it's not the best way to approach your small group conversations.

When you try to **control** your small group conversation . . .
it's difficult to adjust or improvise.
your way becomes the right way.
your questions usually have right answers.
you don't view disagreement as an option.
your few may follow you . . . but not willingly.

But there's a second way to approach your small group conversations.

SGLs who have learned how to lead—rather than control—a small group conversation still know where they're headed and how to get there. But they're comfortable with detours, Dorito stops, and taking the scenic route. They know not everyone will arrive at their destination at the same time, and they understand they'll sometimes need to completely change where they're going. But no matter where they're headed, they're committed to leading their few toward their destination—even if it takes a little longer to get there than originally planned.

When you **lead** your few in a small group conversation . . .
you can manage rabbit trails.
you admit you don't have all the answers.
your questions are open-ended.
you encourage discussion and debate.
you value their opinions and ideas.
your few follow you willingly.

As an SGL, we understand the temptation to want to push your few toward the destination in every conversation. With so much at stake, it makes sense. But here's the bad news. You can't actually control your few. So when you make room for sidetracks, debates, and left turns, you recognize that, while you can't control your few, you can still lead them.

But maybe all this talk about detours and Doritos® has made you a little uneasy (or hungry). Maybe you're wondering how, exactly, to go about leading a small group conversation without controlling it.

We're so glad you asked.

It's not always easy to give up control. But if you want to engage your few in a better small group conversation, you'll need to become a better leader—not a controller— of your small group conversations. And that starts with the kinds of questions you ask. So here are three things you can do to **control less and lead more.**

1. ASK BETTER QUESTIONS

In case no one has told you this already, let us be the ones to break it to you.
As an SGL, your job is not to be an answer giver.
Your job is to be a question asker.

That's a relief, right? You don't actually have to give correct answers to every question a teenage girl asks as though you're a walking, talking, biblical encyclopedia. If the job of a small group leader was to have all the right answers, your volunteer application process probably should've been a lot more difficult.

If it hasn't already happened, one of your few will eventually ask you a difficult question. If you don't have a perfect answer, it's okay to say, "I don't know."

But since your job is to be a question asker, here's an even better idea. Even if you *do* have the perfect answer to that tricky question, don't always give an answer. Instead, ask more questions.

As an SGL, questions are your most important tool. A good question can help you . . .
learn about your few.
understand their perspectives.
make them think.
take them on a journey.

And a good question will help your few . . .
clarify their beliefs.
reconsider their perspectives.
change their opinions.
identify a next step.

So since the questions you ask are such an important tool, let's talk about how to ask the right ones—questions that don't *control* your few, but *lead* them somewhere.

Questions that **control** are questions whose answers are often . . .
one word.
fact-based.
yes or no.
right or wrong.

They're questions like . . .
Did you like the talk this week?
Is gossip a sin?
Who was the apostle Paul?
Don't you agree that _____?

But then there are *better* questions—questions that
lead your few toward your destination, but don't control
their journey.

These questions don't ask for answers. They invite
responses. These questions . . .
are open-ended.
are opinion-based.
invite feedback.
don't have a right answer.

They are questions like . . .
What would it look like if you _____?
What do you think about _____?
What do you think would happen if _____?
What's one thing you can do this week to _____?

In a small group conversation, the best kinds of questions
are questions that ask your few to share their experiences,
their opinions, their observations, and their ideas. They're
questions that expect disagreement and encourage
discussion. And they're questions that invite your few to
think, debate, and come to conclusions together. That's
what it looks like for your few to engage in a conversation
instead of just participate in one. If those aren't the kind of
questions that came in your email, that's okay! You read it
ahead of time and you're able to make some changes.

So if you want to better engage your few by controlling
less and leading more, start by **asking better questions.**

2. VALUE SILENCE

This may be difficult to believe, but it's true. Silence in
a small group conversation can actually be your friend.
Seriously! Sometimes a little silence is exactly what
you need.

Okay, we know. Silence in a small group can be awkward.
If you ask a question and no one responds within three
seconds, you might sometimes go into a mental tailspin.
Was that a stupid question?
Did it even make sense?
Why aren't they talking?
They're never going to talk.
This is a disaster.
Do they all hate me?

Sure, sometimes your group will be silent because you
asked a dumb question. But most of the time, your
question was probably just fine.

Don't rush to fill the silence with an answer or a quick
change of subject. If you can get comfortable with silence,
you can use it. Let them . . .
sit.
think.
process.

And while you wait . . .
gather your thoughts.
watch their body language.
check the clock.
breathe.

When silence sets in, time moves slowly. Ten seconds might
feel like five minutes—especially if you're uncomfortable.
Chances are, your few are just as uncomfortable with the
silence as you are. If you can be patient, someone will
break the silence. So after you ask the question, give

them fifteen seconds to respond. If no one has spoken up after fifteen seconds, then you might want to think about rephrasing your question. But before you dive in to rescue them from the silence, give it time.

When I (Crystal) was a new small group leader, I wanted to teach my few *everything* I knew about God (and I was pretty sure I knew a lot). If there was silence, I took it as a cue that they didn't know the answer and wanted me to jump right in. Eventually I discovered that they were actually waiting to talk because they were trying to be polite (oops). And, because they'd never seen the questions before, it would take a few seconds for them to process what I was asking. So I began to bring a water bottle each week. I would ask a small group question and force myself to take a drink while I waited on the girls to respond. Then if one girl responded, I took another drink while waiting on another. The few seconds it took to chug some water were enough to keep me from answering the question myself (and keep me hydrated).

Try to challenge yourself to wait after asking a question before you speak. If you pay attention, you might even learn something during those 30 seconds of unspeakable torture. Do they look like they're thinking? That's a good thing! Do they look confused? You may need to reword your question. Are they all avoiding eye contact? The question may be too personal. Are they smirking or glancing nervously at each other? You may have uncovered a topic they talk about outside of small group but are embarrassed to talk about inside of small group.

Leading a small group conversation isn't easy when you feel like you're getting the silent treatment. But if you want to better engage your few in conversation by controlling less and leading more, learn to **value silence.**

3. UNDERREACT

Sometimes it's the silence of your few that causes you stress. Other times, one of your few will say something so shocking that you'd happily trade it for an entire day of awkward silence.

Because controlling less and leading more can be risky.

When you
ask questions that are open-ended,
welcome their opinions and feedback,
and encourage discussion and debate,
you won't always be able to anticipate what they'll say
(especially in middle school).

And if your small group is a place where your few feel safe enough to be honest, your questions might actually prompt someone to be honest.

Honest about what she thinks.
Honest about what she believes.
Honest about what she's done.

When one of your few says something in group that surprises you, you might feel like you've lost control.

You haven't.

Take a breath.
Freak out on the inside.
Thank her for sharing.
And ask more questions.

But when one of your few shares something shocking, there's one question you should avoid asking: *Why?*
Why do you think that?
Why don't you believe that?
Why did you do that?

Asking *why* might feel like a reflex. It will be on the tip of your tongue. When a teenager confesses something that shocks you, *why* will seem like the right thing to ask.

When you ask *why*—especially immediately after a teenager has opened up to you—you may lose your opportunity to have a conversation. And without a conversation, you will lose your opportunity to lead her somewhere new.

That's because the question *why* shuts down a conversation. It makes them feel stupid, judged, or ashamed. The same is true for adults. Chances are if we do something wrong, we know it's wrong. So, when we hear *why*, we feel like we're being judged. We want to defend ourselves. We want to put up walls.

That doesn't mean you shouldn't ask *any* questions. It just means you should ask different questions—maybe questions that don't start with *why*. Like . . .
How do you feel about what happened?
What led you to this decision?
What kind of impact do you think this will have on your life, your relationships, or your faith?
What advice would you give someone else in the same situation?

When you decide not to ask *why*, even when you're freaking out on the inside, you invite a conversation, instead of shutting it down.
When you avoid asking *why*, you . . .
show curiosity instead of judgment.
seek to understand instead of being understood.
choose to listen instead of panic.

When you underreact instead of overreact, you prove to your few that your small group really is a safe place. And you can also model for your few what grace and compassion look like so *they* will know how to respond when a friend tells them something shocking. Because if you want your few to engage in your small group conversation, you'll need to help them see your group is a safe place to talk about anything—even the things that shock you.

So if you want your small group conversations to matter more, ask better questions, value silence, and underreact. And remember that you're not the small group controller. You're the small group leader. So **control less, lead more.**

QUIZ:

HOW WELL DO YOU LEAD YOUR FEW?

This is what makes an SGL different than a Sunday school teacher—you've got to be a master conversationalist. And you've chosen to be a leader. So, you've got to keep learning to master the art of group talk. Here are a few quick questions to see how well you lead your group.

When was the last time your group felt out of control? What happened?

....

....

....

Have you ever held your group hostage while you discussed every single question on your small group guide?

....

....

....

QUIZ

What's the best conversation your few have had in group recently? What sparked the conversation?

When was the last time your small group went silent? How did you handle it?

Next time one of your few shares something shocking, what's one thing you can do to be sure you under-react (besides practicing your best poker face in the mirror)?

NEXT STEP

We know the art of LEADING looks different for everyone. Below, write one or two specific and practical things you can do to better LEAD a conversation with your few this week.

4.3

If you want your small group conversations to matter more,

script less, improvise more.

(Let's talk about your plan.)

script less, improvise more

As you prepare for your small group conversation each week, you probably have an idea in mind of how the conversation will go. That's great! Having a plan is an important part of preparing for your small group conversation. But as you prepare, rehearse, and read your small group questions in advance, keep in mind:

There's no script for a small group conversation.
At some point, things will not go according to plan.
And you will probably have to improvise.

If your small group experience is anything like ours, you know that even the tiniest distraction can derail a group. I (Crystal) live in the South, and it only snows here a couple of times a year. So, snow isn't a tiny distraction for students or adults. It's an all-out event. Several years ago, I was leading a group when fluffy, white flakes started falling outside. In the middle of my oh-so-prepared small group questions, my girls jumped up, left our circle, ran to the window, and started shouting with joy.

I contemplated letting them celebrate for a few minutes and then jumping back into our small group questions, but before I could even complete the thought, I heard a loud collective *BUZZ*. Every girl got a notification that school had just been cancelled for the next day. There was no turning back. We had gone from "let's talk about the value of prayer," to total and complete mayhem in the span of 10 seconds. It was a moment of "if you can't beat the chaos, join it." I tossed my questions aside, grabbed a coat and invited my girls to a dance party in the snow. We laughed, took pictures, danced to music played from our cell phones, and ultimately didn't answer another single question that night. It wasn't my plan, but it's still one of our favorite memories.

There's a principle in improv comedy called the "Yes, and . . . " principle. The idea is the comedian will see whatever situation, no matter how absurd, no matter how impossible, and say yes. They won't quit. They won't try to force the situation to be more rational. They simply jump in and roll with it. They say *yes* (either verbally or inwardly), and then build on whatever is already happening.

It starts by saying "Yes." When you say *yes*, you agree to accept whatever situation, story, or energy the rest of your group throws your way.

"Yes, I am dressed like a hot dog."
"Yes, we are on the moon."
"Yes, I am a little grumpy today."

And when you take your "Yes" a step further by saying, "Yes, and . . . " you not only accept what's been thrown at you, but you also build on it.

Like this . . .
"Yes, I am dressed like a hot dog, and I'm also late for my doctor's appointment."
"Yes, we are on the moon, and hey—it's made of ice cream!"
"Yes, I am a little grumpy, but that's because my eyebrows are missing."

You probably will never lead a small group while on the moon or dressed like a hot dog. (But I've seen the kinds of games student pastors play, so maybe that whole missing your eyebrows situation is not *all* that unrealistic.) But here's the point. If you want to engage your few in better conversations, you're going to need to be ready to improvise—to take whatever your few throw at you, and then build on it.

Most of the time, you'll only need to improvise a little.
Like when a question isn't working.
Or your few are too fidgety.
Or too talkative.
Or you have a first-time visitor.

But other times, you may need to throw away your plan entirely.
Like when 20 girls show up.
Or only one girl shows up.
Or your entire group is fighting.
Or one of your few experiences a tragedy.

As SGLs who have been forced to improvise more times than we can count, we want to tell *you* something we wish someone had told *us*.

You're allowed to improvise.
In fact, you should probably plan on it.

Because if you want to engage your few in a better small group conversation, you'll need to get comfortable with being uncomfortable. And that starts by letting go of your plan, saying "Yes, and . . . " and choosing to **script less, improvise more.**

Here are four ways to do that . . .

1. CHANGE THE QUESTION

You won't always be able to predict the kinds of questions that will work for your small group. Sometimes a question may take you by surprise and start a great conversation. Other times, what you thought was a great conversation starter may result in blank stares and looks of utter confusion.

Sometimes your few might have trouble responding to one of your open-ended questions. That could be because the question is confusing, or maybe it's just because they're a little tired that day. But if your few are having trouble answering an open-ended question, go ahead—change the question.

Here's an example.

Let's say your few are struggling to respond to the question, "How close do you feel to God right now?" Maybe the question was a little *too* open ended. Maybe they're not sure how to put their responses into words. If they're having difficulty, ask the question again. But this time, give them a few options to choose from, like: "On a scale of 1-5, how close do you feel to God right now?"

In a small group conversation, open-ended questions are usually best. But when your few are struggling to respond, turning an open-ended question into a multiple-choice question can help narrow their options.

Or maybe the problem isn't the question. Maybe your few aren't responding because their responses would be too personal, too intimate, or embarrassing. If that's the case, you don't need to throw away the question entirely. You just need to make it a little less personal.

So instead of asking them when was the last time they lied, you might say, "Tell me about a time someone lied to you."

Or instead of asking which sin tempts them the most, you could ask, "What's one thing people your age are often tempted by?" If that still doesn't work, try asking about how a similar situation played out in one of their favorite books or movies. Teenagers aren't always good at talking about themselves, but they're usually great at talking about other people.

In a small group conversation, it's good to ask tough questions. But when a question seems a little *too* tough for your few, making the question feel a little less personal can get the conversation moving again.

No matter how much you plan for your small group, your small group conversation can't be scripted. That's why it's so important to improvise. So if you want to better engage your few by scripting less and improvising more, **change a question** or two. You have permission!

2. TRY AN ACTIVITY

Sometimes changing a question is all the improvisation you'll need to help your conversation get unstuck. But other times, you may need to try something a little more drastic. Okay, maybe drastic isn't the right word. We don't mean to scare you.

But on the weeks when your group is too talkative, not talkative, silly, restless, or distracted, you might want to move away from your typical conversation and try something more hands-on like an activity.

Maybe you've already improvised by changing an open-ended question into a scale question, like "On a scale of 1-5, how close do you feel to God right now?" To turn that scale question into an activity, you might try this: "On a scale of *this* wall to *that* wall, stand in the place that represents how close you feel to God right now."

Or you could hand out pens and paper. Then ask your few to write down their responses to a question or two. When they're finished writing, you could . . .
read their responses out loud.
ask them to read their own responses out loud.
post them on a wall or bulletin board.

Or you can make a small group video about what you've been learning. Ask each of your few to share what they're learning in 30 seconds or less. Then use your phone to edit their clips into a complete video.

Or you might decide to break up the group dynamics by splitting into pairs. When everyone has a partner, spend time praying together or discussing questions one at a time.

Or maybe you ask your few to work together on a project, challenge, or action step together. Give them something tangible to do that helps them personalize the topic you're discussing.

Or maybe you decide that, this week, the best thing you can do to love, influence, and care for your few is to throw away all of your small group questions and play a game instead.

While activities might look different for every small group, remember you have the freedom to improvise. Because here's the good news—the point of your small group conversation isn't to make it through every discussion question. The point is to help your few engage in a conversation about authentic faith so they can better live out authentic faith. So if you want to better engage your few by scripting less and improvising more, **try an activity!**

SMALL GROUP SURVIVAL KIT:
PENS & PAPER
This survival kit item might be the most
important of all. When your conversation just
isn't working well, hand out paper and pens
to everyone! You can choose to use these
however you think works best, but you might
want to try asking them to write down their
responses on paper and giving them back
to you. Another option is that they could
write down the numbers 1-5, and circle the
answer they choose. Or maybe they just need
something to do with their hands while they
talk, and doodling is the perfect solution.

3. FOLLOW RABBIT TRAILS

There will be weeks when everything seems to be going
well. Your few are engaging in the conversation. The
questions seem to be working. The conversation is moving.

There will also be weeks when the conversation will take a
turn you didn't expect. Maybe it's prompted by something
someone said, or by what the group nearby just shouted,
or by a text that just came in, or by absolutely nothing at
all. No matter where the interruption comes from, it's true
that more often than you'd probably like, your small group
conversation will be derailed by a rabbit trail.

Rabbit trails are funny little things, and the good ones will
stick with you long after that small group conversation
has ended. I (Ashley) vividly remember the first time I
encountered one in my middle school small group that I
simply could not control. It went a little like this:
"I never really thought about how Jesus actually died. Like,
He *really* died."
"Like the dead groundhog I saw on the way here!"
"I saw a dead chicken on the way here!"

"Did you know if you cut off a chicken's head, the body can keep running?"
"We chicken-sat for our neighbors last year."
"Did you know chickens sometimes eat their own eggs?"
"My friend told me that chickens sometimes eat each other."

Yeah, I'm still not sure how I could have recovered from that one.

If the rabbit trails that pop up in your small group are about chickens . . . or boys . . . or the video they just saw on YouTube, it's okay to shut those conversations down so you can keep things moving.

But sometimes you'll come across a rabbit trail that's actually worth following.

Maybe Jewel will ask a question.
Or Samri will share something that's been happening at school.
Or Bria will tell you her mom is sick.

Not every rabbit trail is worth following, but if the rabbit trail you're dealing with . . .
is timely
is important
sparks their interest
. . . then pursue it.

Because if you want to better engage your few by scripting less and improvising more, sometimes you'll need to **follow the rabbit trail.**

4. GO WITH YOUR GUT

Okay, maybe the idea of improvising makes you nervous. Maybe you like—no, *love*—having a plan. Maybe you're nervous about moving away from the plan your student pastor gives you. Maybe you're worried you don't have permission.

If that's you, here's something to keep in mind.

No one knows your few like you know your few. Not even your student pastor.

Week after week, you are the person who . . .
connects with them,
knows them,
and engages with them.
You know their lives, their worlds, their quirks, and their backgrounds.

And since you know your few so well, it's up to you to customize your small group conversations so they work for your small group. We can give you some ideas, and your student pastor can give you some helpful questions. But the truth is, it's up to you. If you're going to learn to script less and improvise more, you're going to have to trust your gut, experiment, and sometimes even fail. That's okay. Sometimes you learn more from failing than you do from succeeding. Don't be afraid of it.

No one can tell you exactly how to lead your small group. Only you can do that.

So trust yourself. Because if you want to better engage your few by scripting less and improvising more, you don't need an instruction manual. You need to go with your gut.

After you've prepared, connected, and gotten to know your few, if you want your small group conversations to matter more, you're going to have to engage them in a conversation. But not just any conversation—a conversation about authentic faith. That's why it's so important you learn to **speak less and listen more, control less and lead more, script less and improvise more.**

Because before a teenager can ENGAGE in a *life* of authentic faith, she may need to ENGAGE in a *conversation* about authentic faith.

QUIZ:

HOW WELL DO YOU IMPROVISE WITH YOUR FEW?

This is the good old fashioned "bob and weave." ~~Sometimes~~ *All the time* you need to be flexible in your role as a small group leader. Here are a few questions to see just how flexible you can be!

On a scale of one to breaking-out-in-a-vicious-sweat, how uncomfortable are you with going off-script in a small group conversation?

Sweating and
hyperventilating

Rolling with
the punches

1   2   3   4   5

What are some small group questions that have totally bombed?

QUIZ

What's one way you've learned to improvise when your small group script isn't working?

Have you ever completely thrown away your script? What happened?

QUIZ

What's the best rabbit trail you've ever followed?

NEXT STEP

We know the art of IMPROVISING looks different for everyone. Below, write one or two specific and practical tricks you can use to IMPROVISE when you need to shift your group conversation.

5

chapter
five
move

Move

Congratulations! You did it! You successfully engaged your small group of teenage girls in a conversation about authentic faith!

Well, not really. You're reading a book right now. You're not leading a small group.

But let's *pretend* you've been leading a successful conversation with your small group.

And now let's imagine you're ready to wrap up that conversation.

Sure, you could wrap things up by yelling, "Okay, we're done, bye!" and sprinting for the door.

But we know you. We know you care about making your small group conversations matter more. In fact, we're pretty sure you care so much about making your small group conversations matter that you wouldn't just throw it all away in the last few moments of your time together. You're going to be strategic. You're going to finish strong.

Because it's great to engage your few in a conversation about authentic faith, but leading small group conversations isn't the only reason you signed up to be a small group leader, is it? You signed up to be a small group leader because you wanted . . .
to make a big difference.
to change the world.
to invest in a few teenage girls so that you could help them develop a lifelong, authentic kind of faith.

That's why we know you won't wrap up your small group conversation by lunging for the door.

Once you've engaged your few in a *conversation* about authentic faith, your final step is to **move your few to engage in a *life* of authentic faith.** In other words, after you've engaged them *inside* your circle, it's your job to move them to engage *outside* your circle.

So before you move for the door, here are three ways to keep your few moving toward authentic faith—even after the conversation has ended.

If you want to move your few, GIVE a next step.

When we talked about leading—not controlling—your small group conversations, we talked about the importance of keeping the end in mind. Your ultimate . . .
destination
target
finish-line
goal
. . . isn't necessarily to help your few *remember* what they've heard. As their small group leader, your goal is to help them *apply* it.

Keep that goal in mind as you wrap up your small group conversation each week. Before you move your few out of your circle and back into the world, give them a next step. When you help them identify one simple step they can take during the week, you'll help your few learn to not only *talk* about their faith, but to *live* it out, too. So wrap up your conversation each week by asking, "What's *one* thing you're going to do this week to live this out?"

Then be sure to follow up. In a group text, ask them how it's going, or remind them of how they can live out what they're learning. Not only is it a great reminder, but your few will become used to the idea that what they're learning at church is meant to carry over into the rest of the week.

Remember, when you give a next step, you move them toward action.

If you want to move your few, PRAY together.

You may not always have time in small group to hear from every girl about every prayer request she's ever had, but you do have time to close in prayer. Some weeks, everyone might have the opportunity to pray. Other weeks, you may only have time for one, but whether you have ten minutes or ten seconds for prayer, don't forget to pray together.

Get in the habit of asking your few for prayer requests.
Then write down their prayer requests.
And follow up on their prayer requests.

When you pray for, and with, your few, you're modeling what it looks like to talk to God, to know God, and to trust God. Imagine the impact you could have on a teenage girl's faith if your weekly small group conversations helped her have better conversations, not just with her small group, but with the God who made her.

Because when you pray together, you move them toward God.

When I (Ashley) asked my small group to pray together for the first time, it didn't go well. No one made eye contact. No one volunteered. It kind of seemed like everyone wanted to melt into the carpet.

I guess I shouldn't have been that surprised. Praying out loud in a small group can be weird, especially if you don't know each other very well. After a few months, I tried again. This time, I *strongly* encouraged them to pray. They looked terrified, so I gave them an out. I told them that if they didn't know what to say, they could simply say, "God, thank you for being you. And thank you for our small group." And they did. All of them. For months.

And then one week, one brave girl decided to try something new. She prayed from her heart. She didn't need my words at all. The following week, her friends did the same, because that's how teenage girls work. Within a few weeks, everyone had so much to say to God that we had to extend our small group time. I was so proud of them! They got there, but it took time.

If you want to move your few, SAY something meaningful.

If you've led well, you've probably spent most of your small group conversation asking questions, listening, and asking more questions. But as your small group conversation comes to a close, and your few are preparing to leave the safe place of your small group for another week, you have the opportunity to say something meaningful—something that has the potential to stay with them all week long.

Like . . .
"I love you."
"I'm praying for you."
"I'm proud of you."
"I'm here for you."
"I believe in you."

When you say something meaningful to your few, you help them feel significant. Who knows the impact those words might have on even one teenage girl in your group. Every compliment counts. After all, a few words can make a big difference in the direction of someone's life. When you take your time at the end of group, you are showing them that no matter what they did or said in group, you still love them and you're still *for them*. And that means they're more likely to come back and engage next week.

So before you move your few out of your circle, choose
your words wisely. Say something meaningful. When you
do, you'll move them toward *feeling* as significant as you
already know they are.

If you want to move your few, MOVE WITH THEM.

We get it. You're a busy person, and after your group
conversation is over you have . . .
a dinner to heat up in the microwave.
a spouse to see.
a roommate to chat with.
a day job to prep for.
a life to get back to.

But before you bolt for your car, make sure you don't miss
a huge opportunity. The few minutes after group are one of
the most strategic times to connect with individual girls in
your group. Maybe you need to . . .
follow up on one of their answers during group.
clarify what she meant when she said something surprising.
explain something *you* meant when it came out differently
than you intended.
encourage her.
ask about her mom or her math test or her pet frog.

As you wrap up your small group conversation, remember
to finish strong. When you give a next step, pray together,
say something meaningful, and walk out with them, you
help your few move—not just out of your circle, but into a
life of more authentic faith.

conclusion

Conclusion

If you are a middle school small group leader, you have about 156 small groups over the course of the three years of middle school.

If you are a high school small group leader, you have about 200 small groups over the course of the four years of high school.

You can make every single one of them count.
And you can make every single one of them matter.
And just like every individual conversation, they'll all go better if you start with the end in mind.

Just imagine . . .

Three years from now, your sweet now-sixth-grade girl will walk into the world of high school. In a whole new world, she'll be exposed to pressures and experiences she has only seen in movies. She'll face challenges that she couldn't have imagined back in sixth grade. And she'll be ready because she took with her 156 conversations that gave her wisdom, encouragement, and beliefs.

Four years from now, your spunky now-ninth-grade girl will walk onto her college campus. In a whole new world without mom or dad or your church, she'll face challenges that she couldn't have imagined back in ninth grade. And she'll be ready because she took with her 200 conversations that gave her wisdom, belonging, and faith.

When she feels lost, your group memories may just push her to find friends who share her faith.

When she encounters doubts, she may just call someone in your group because it's always been a safe place to ask tough questions.

And when she stands in all the noise of a new school, there's a good chance she'll still hear YOUR voice in the back of her mind reminding her to . . .
make the wise choice.
put others first.
trust God.
find community.
pray.

Your conversation this week matters.

And it can matter more in light of all those conversations added together.

So if you want to have better conversations with the teenage girls in your small group . . .
PREPARE for the conversation you'll have in your circle.
CONNECT with your few, and help them connect with each other.
KNOW your few, and help them know each other.
ENGAGE your few by speaking less, listening more, controlling less, leading more, scripting less and improvising more.
MOVE your few toward a life of authentic faith outside your circle.

That's not easy. Leading conversations with teenage girls can still be difficult, no matter how well you prepare, connect, know, engage, or move your few. Sometimes . . .
they'll still be distracted.
you'll still ask a question that falls flat.

they'll still sit in silence.
you'll still lose control.
they'll still ask questions you can't answer.
you'll still wonder who put you in charge.

We probably haven't answered all of your questions.
We probably haven't solved all of your problems.
But we hope we've shared at least a few stories, ideas, and
strategies that will help you make your next small group
conversation a little more effective.

So this week . . .
Prepare
Connect
Know
Engage
Move

And remember . . .

Every conversation with your small group matters.
But you can make this week's conversation matter
even more.

author
bios

Author bios

ASHLEY BOHINC

Ashley serves as the Director of Middle School Strategy at Orange. She has worked with students in public education, athletic, and ministry settings since 2005. Ashley is most passionate about resourcing the local church, communicating on stage, developing leaders, working with students, and world missions. Additionally, she is the USA Director of Carry 117, a ministry in Ethiopia, which focuses on orphan prevention and family preservation by empowering women. In her downtime, you'll find her watching *Friends*, cheering on the Cleveland Cavaliers, traveling, or on one of her Fairytale Friday Adventures.

CRYSTAL CHIANG

Crystal Chiang is the Director of XP3 High School Curriculum. Before joining the team at Orange, she spent 10 years as a high school Spanish teacher and student ministry leader, doing everything from small groups to speaking to curriculum design. She currently volunteers at her church as a leader to sophomore girls whose numbers are creating what might be deemed a not-so-small group. They keep her laughing, praying, and constantly on her toes. Crystal and her husband, Tom, live in Atlanta, GA with their embarrassingly ill-tempered chihuahua, Javier.

LEARN MORE
ABOUT LEAD SMALL
+
DOWNLOAD OUR
UBERCOOL AMAZING
FREE APP
@ LEADSMALL.ORG